www.hants.gov.uk/library

Dorothy Wordsworth's Christmas Birthday

Carol Ann Duffy

Illustrated by Tom Duxbury

PICADOR

First published 2014 by Picador
an imprint of Pan Macmillan, a division of Macmillan Publishers Limited
Pan Macmillan, 20 New Wharf Road, London N1 9RR
Basingstoke and Oxford
Associated companies throughout the world
www.panmacmillan.com

ISBN 978-1-4472-7150-5

For Pamela Woof
And all at The Wordsworth Trust

Dorothy Wordsworth's Christmas Birthday

First, frost at midnight –
Moon, Venus and Jupiter
named in their places.

Ice, like a cold key,
turning its lock on the lake;
nervous stars trapped there.

Darkness, a hand poised
over the chord of the hills;
the strange word *moveless*.

The landscape muted;
soft apprehension of snow,
a holding of breath.

Up, rapt at her gate,
Dorothy Wordsworth ages
one year in an hour;

her Christmas birthday
inventoried by an owl,
clock-eyed, time-keeper.

Indoors, the thrilled fire
unwraps itself; sprightly hands
opening the coal.

For she cannot sleep,
Dorothy, primed with herself,
waiting for morning . . .

gradual sure light,
like the start of a poem,
its local accent.

Striding towards dawn,
Samuel Taylor Coleridge
swigs at his port wine,

sings a nonsense rhyme,
which Helm Crag learns and echoes
at the speed of sound.

The rock formations –
old lady at piano,
a lion, a lamb.

And, out on a limb,
he skids down a silvered lane
into a sunburst;

a delight of bells,
the exact mood of his heart,
from St. Oswald's Church.

New rime on the grass
where the Wordsworths' graves will be
at another time.

Not there, then; here, now,
Dorothy's form on the road
coming to meet him,

in her claret frock,
in her boots, bonnet and shawl,
her visible breath.

Then her arm through his
on the stroll to Dove Cottage;
spiced apples baking.

Wordsworth lies a-bed
in his nightshirt and nightcap,
rhyming *cloud* with *crowd*.

The cat at his feet
licks at her black-and-white fur,
rhyming *purr* with *purr*.

The kitchen table,
set for this festive breakfast,
an unseen still-life:

cream in a brown jug,
the calmness of bowls and spoons,
one small round white loaf.

And a tame robin,
aflame on the windowsill,
its name in its song.

They walk to the lake,
where Wordsworth skates like a boy,
in heaven on earth;

a tangerine sun
illuminating the hour
into manuscript;

so Dorothy's gifts
are the gold outlines of hills,
are emblazoned trees;

Coleridge on a rock,
lighting his pipe, votive smoke
ascending the air . . .

Nowt to show more fair –
ecstatic, therefore, her stare,
seeing it all in.

Later, the lamps lit
in the parlour, hot punch fumes
in a copper pan.

The feast: mutton pie,
buttered parsnips, potatoes,
a Halifax goose.

Coleridge's flushed face,
never so vivid again
in Dorothy's mind.

Loud boots at the porch
and a stout thump on the door
as the Minstrels come,

dangling their tin cans
for a free ladle of ale
after caroling . . .

Bring us in good ale,
for that goes down at once-oh!
Bring us in good ale . . .

All in each other,
Miss Wordsworth and the poets,
bawling the chorus;

their voices drifting,
in 1799,
to nowhen, nowhere . . .

but Winter's slow turn,
and snow in Dorothy's hair
and on her warm tongue.

Also by Carol Ann Duffy and available from Picador